CLEARWA`

MW01483344

T 19822

# In The Slow Twilight
# of the Standing Stones:

# The Barra Poems

| | DATE DUE | | |
|---|---|---|---|
| | | | |
| | | | |
| | | | |
| | | | |
| | | | |
| | | | |
| | | | |
| | | | |
| | | | |
| | | | |
| | | | |
| | | | |

# In The Slow Twilight
# of the Standing Stones

## The Barra Poems

## Florence McNeil

Ekstasis  Editions

National Library of Canada Cataloguing in Publication Data

McNeil, Florence
    In the slow twilight of the standing stones: the barra poems


    Poems.
    ISBN 1-896860-95-8
    PS8525.N43I5 2001        C811'.54        C2001-911167-3
    PR9199.3.M336I5 2001

Published in 2001 by:
Ekstasis Editions Canada Ltd.                    Ekstasis Editions
Box 8474, Main Postal Outlet                         Box 571
Victoria, B.C. V8W 3S1                        Banff, Alberta ToL oCo

*In the Slow Twilight of the Standing Stones: The Barra Poems* has been published
with the assistance of a grant from the Canada Council for the Arts and the Cultural
Services Branch of British Columbia.

*This book is dedicated to two wonderful Hebridean women: Mary (Gilles) Chappell and Jessie (MacNeil) MacLellan,who brought to their new country their gifts of laugher, kindness, warmth and determination — with love.*

# Preface

In the early 1920's my grandparents were among the emigrants from the Scottish Hebridean island of Barra who came to Canada as part of a Canadian Pacific Railway land scheme. They were small crofters recruited to farm the huge empty acres of Alberta, and most, after experiencing the first winter came to Vancouver. They settled, mainly in the same area, and were in constant contact with one another, so I grew up hearing Gaelic, listening to poems and songs, taking part in highland dancing. The culture of Barra was oral—the island is the most southern and westerly of the Outer Hebrides, so far away from the mainland that until lately it was almost isolated. The island became a treasure trove of customs, rituals, stories, poetry and music handed down through the succession of civilizations from the Neolithic age, through the times of the Druids, Celts and Vikings in long, unbroken waves of assimilations. The inhabitants moved easily from the druidic age to the Christian, partly because the monks who brought Christianity to the island were wise men, able to work with the existing beliefs. The northern half of the outer Hebrides gradually became strict Protestant; the southern half has remained Catholic. As a result, in Barra there was never a division between enjoyment and religion (the celtic afterworld was depicted as a huge feast), the pubs were always full, the statues never removed from the churches.

Barra is the home of the McNeils. Kisimul Castle, now restored, sits on a rock outcroppping in the bay, appearing to arise from the water. The castle's most distinguished appendage, Kisimul Galley, in Elizabethan times, was renowned for speed and daring, for fighting and plundering and for miraculous escapes.

At present, Barra is a mecca for summer visitors. The Gaelic signs are everywhere, and during the summer festival there are lessons in the harp, in the language, in dancing and history. I visited Barra in the 90's, and this is my record.

I was aware at all times that I was home, among my people. The culture I knew growing up in Burnaby (outside Vancouver) had its origin here. Watching my parents, grandparents, and relatives balancing the new demands of Canada, holding on to what they knew, instilled in me the sense of belonging to two cultures. The old people I knew as a child are all gone, but their counterparts live on the island. Names are mentioned—you are someone's daughter, granddaughter—the whole panoply of the past surrounds you, is still living.

I have taken liberties in writing this poetic memoir. I chose St. Columba, whose skill and courage was documented in his own time, to represent all the monks who travelled to the islands—often alone in small skin-covered boats: the coracles. The "dark people" represent the earliest inhabitants—the origins. They were thought to be small; they preceded the druids, celts and vikings by thousands of years. When I was in Barra the archaeologists were uncovering a Viking village; later they were to discover traces of this neolithic civilization—in the deep recesses of the island. They represent, in my book, the roots of the Barra people, of my own discoveries. I have used the imagery of Celtic art to suggest the interconnectedness of the islander's lives.

These people who absorbed the changes of the centuries with irony, tolerance, humour, and an unshakable sense of the marvellous, were able to transfer their gifts to Canada. Like the art, there is no beginning and no end.

# First Lines

The plane grazes these islands
looming out of a thousand year mist
chained together   in the north Atlantic
they belong to me
and the small one with its scribbled indentations
barely visible now
holds my life story.

St. Columba would have liked the airport chapel
he had praying sites for voyages
coming and going
where he knelt in silence
reflecting on the ocean
with its corners beyond vision
the lines he must not cross
the struggle for the sky
the coracle flimsy and insignificant
the daylight stars
that had no light
until a clump of rocks swaddled by the ocean
could give him rest
the western isles so far away he could cover them
with his palm
And reaching up he prayed the
ocean might recede
And the night lost its small moon
and heather appeared beneath his head
and he slept
In the morning the coracle shone
the islands floated near
he bathed in salt
and sang in thanksgiving

This chapel is stark
a celtic blessing welcomes me
its script connected
forward and backwards   encompassing
the growing word
the last command.

The ship pulls in toward
    the castle
which has risen for me
so far out in the bay
it is more sea than land
the pictures I have
studied all my life
the calendars from my grandmother's kitchen
the postcards
old scenes where the sea is ink
and the bruised people
the colour of the earth
and having known it all my life
torn from someone else's lens
I cannot comprehend it now
the tide is low   there are the ancient
rocks
the square turrets
and brown people coming through
the opening
and in the last fissure of the sun
I photograph the castle
placing it backwards
into my mythology.

There have been other islands scattered on
all sides to form a continuum
there is a rough crossing
the benign fingers are left behind
and I am tossed back into my history
surging towards the vikings   the celts   picts
the dark vibrant people who lived
far out in the imagination
separated from stillness   there is a raging
hill encompassing other hills
and the grey indentations with sheep
painted in the background
we pull into port   are docked
as the ancient galley long ago tethered by
this castle
I am alone   it is late   the days
still lingering at 10 o'clock
arriving as
my family left   with tears in my eyes.

I pass them at the pier they are pulling out
It is 1923
they are tilting the rail   they are waving
and the crowds below the primroses
the neat fences bordered with sheep
It is April   white handkerchiefs   white waves and
the dark crying people
watching each other   there is more here than death
out of this world that grows weaker and more
insignificant the slow absorption into the ocean
I was sick for days   my mother said
that was all I knew
they had erased my home
someone took away my childhood
and I was never safe

we pull in nearer and nearer
the night sun outlines the shimmering
castle
this island is the last one   the outer limits
circled forever in the huge anger
of the Atlantic
where the wind and the rains that sheer the heather
fill the air with cyclic tunes

barely tamable  even in spring

and yet as we make dock   I understand the words
enveloped by the yellow green hills   the people at the
pier waving at us  splashed by the last gaudy sun
and everyone is reaching towards me   and compelling my testimony.

Orchids   violets   yellow iris
meadow-mist worn by
Cuchulain the druid
as a talisman towards abundance
Before the first world war
the herring a dance of phosphorescent light
around the island
till the circle diminished
and the fish boats became postcards
And the grandparents and children
followed the postcards to Canada
leaving in spring as Cuchulain appeared again
and Columba returned from his cell
to repeat the ancient prayers
to bless the lark   the cuckoo   the receding people
They did not know
they were going to a monochromatic land
the last rainbow shining over their island
the piper on the pier
black amongst the thyme and sea pink
smaller than their outstretched hands.

A picture of the emigrants on the ship
untidy   hidden each from the other
no one is standing close
in a movie they would be arranged
by the rails
and one could glimpse
possibilities

It is April   there are pansies and daffodils
on the hills
but the emigrants are bundled from the chill that is to come
my mother   my grandparents are somewhere
there
lost in the shawls and
overcoats
one face is partially clear
a baby in a woollen bonnet
who is held up near the rail by
invisible strings
They are so tied to the picture
they might be slaves crossing against their will
I know this is not so
but for a child   my mother
bereft of choice   there is only the long angle
of the boat and the faces she does
not want to leave

The boat will shake itself loose from the pier
and move its captives on towards
the blue-green silence of the icebergs
a hill where the train slinks and the seasons
have not turned over
the daffodils and tulips
still dead in frozen ground.

The railroad scheme took them through Canada
to the endless landscape of Alberta
I wanted to hide   my mother said
but it was too flat
and you were always looking at it
they had been surrounded by sea
its intricate patterns frightening and consoling
there was no voyage out of this prairie
and no mists
to soften the obtrusive fields
or the sun that shone futilely day after day

In the church hall on the island
they had seen apple orchards and soft fields   tame hills
and young Canadians beckoning them in the
continual fragrance of sunlight

As the mud turned to red clay turned to
solid winter
in a house with holes dotting the walls
and the wind singing English songs
(there were no words in their Gaelic for this experience)
my grandparents put aside the apple trees
the seductive people in the films
and set their sights on the floating coast.

One road circles the island
so narrow our taxi driver
makes excursions into turnarounds
and everyone waves
there are sputtering voices on his machine
my mother   he says
(she is dispatcher   counsellor and
guide)
and sometimes he said she disappears
and I can hear Glasgow or
music
I think of the music as we make our journey
in spring   the small people chant their
welcoming songs
and the lark pours herself out into the
immense stillness
there is music in expressions
which change   as the island changes
from sunshine to unspoken
melancholy
Later my cousin in my father's old home
tells a story
it begins softly   becomes poetry   then song
and I am home in Canada
a small child warmed by the fire
while outside the mountains loom in the dark
and the rain shapes the cedars
I am listening to my parents and my grandparents
rekindle
their songs
and these are my first notes.

In the blackness there were the dark people
who forced stones into driftwood
and worshipped the movement of seasons
they lived among the seals   the mermaids
swam in seaweed
they belonged to an age that is beneath the islands
through the layers of more recent apparitions
they transformed themselves into the celts
who believed more in bribery than in prayer
who made friends with the searing wind
the raging sea
everything named and honoured in a burst of repetitive poetry
they were able to welcome St. Columba and turned their runes into
crosses
the intricate patterns of their carvings
no end   no beginning
their songs now more lyrical
filled with an elaboration--
of shields   of blessings--with one eye on the new god
and their voices chanting in
the exultations of the hills.

At mass the choir sings a Gaelic hymn
I know the tune but its meaning is part
of my childhood church   its wooden spire
echoing the thrust of fir and cedar
and music
there are few trees on this island
and the church is stone upon bolstering stone
like the castle
In Gaelic and English I hear what I
have heard before

there was always another world
spirits for the little people
lost in dark caves holding on to their prayers
St. Columba visiting from Ireland
Christ is my druid he said
So far away   so lost in open sea
the Islanders have knelt and sung
and learned
and it was all one
They welcomed the visitors from the other world
(there were no strangers
the extra place was always set)
Blending into one another   blessing the accretions of time
in the slow twilight of the standing stones.

Exchanging the prairies for the farther west
my grandfather set out to view the coast
leaving the linear fields
the overabundant sky
to tunnel through the rockies
to be delivered to the ocean
to a landscape
redrawn from the island
humps and hollows
emptying into water
a mist falling
    in small dots
the air full
    of swollen hours
And he was home
The Hebrideans came singly
    and in groups   to Vancouver
to live near a bridge
elevating to a mountain
and boats trimming the narrow inlet
They would settle close to one another
holding each other in a web
and the spirits that had travelled with them
close enough
to shut off
the imperative of the city.

In Canada they gave each other gifts
of constant visitation
house to house   by the sea so like their own
English now mingling with Gaelic
in the gathering of news   the telephone
the reading of letters
the deaths   the birth of lambs   of stubborn crops
the storms that hurled themselves above the hills
season to season
and the tales of spirits
wandering even more   looking for the emigrants
the old ones settling their claims
had thickening accents
the young people
preoccupied with movie screens
disguised their speech
but the soft musical notes would not leave
were as integral as their own names
I see them now   I see them
on this island
The people following the piper
are my people
the dancers who consume this night
danced in my living room
The old people pausing between two centuries
applauded as they do tonight
this generous re-enactment
the perfection of memory.

St. Columba like Francis
loved creation
he sailed his coracle to the island
pulling the leather frame
onto the white sand
From the corners the creatures came
their sharp melting eyes
watching from branches
from grass tufts   the heather rippling   finding his altar
Columba blessed the tapestry   this was the beginning
the Islanders quietly assembling before him
loving his soft voice
the muscular arms which
fought the western sea
They knew his god   the extension of their own shields and stone
He would be full of songs and triumph
of delicate interpretations
in the tending of seasons
He would be welcome here.

celtic art I


The archaeologists
are bending over the unclaimed sites
from their fingers small pieces
of some other time
white bones and sand
entangling
it is a slow fall
down the centuries
the minuscule contents
enlarging
and the people who have fallen
deeper
bone upon bone
are creating charts and maps
like a spring river
burgeoning
So many have bent
their backs upon the island
in the time of gathering peat
the ripe potatoes the struggling nets
the wind twisting them so they
were knotted together in their weariness
with the earth
with the ones who
reached toward them
in the perfect circle.

The machair   the strip between sea and land
is plush with wild geraniums yellow cornflowers thyme
and heather tall enough to change shapes in the wind

There is another graveyard past the machair
past the white sands which gleam in the sun
and darkness as the wind and rain intensify
This cemetery is eroding
the graves
returning to the sea and the unquiet walk

These are the urgent   the drowned sailor in the yellow rain gear
watches constantly over a small cottage
visitors have seen him at
the window
his hands rubbing the glass
as if in salute
they felt no fear
he was only visiting they said

Through thousands
of years
they have been appearing and disappearing
they are falling into the sea
and walking once again
filling the air with their own translations
of bird song   wind song.

The holy man walks the island
his staff strikes rocks
that split apart
the dry birds grow their wings
in the changing light
he speaks softly to the
cows   the sheep
who bow before him
in the grove of oak he kneels
(the trees remembering their past
flaunt their leaves
the holy man traces the porous wood)
the rains appear
the doors open
and the islanders take him
into shelter
there is peace now
he is among them
the new druid
the builder of bridges
the fire has never gone out.

I step over the soft long sand
into the aquamarine water
gentle today
yet tentative
there are no definite plans
unlike my own coast on a spring day
(a gentle rain stroking the flower heads
the sun picking itself out of the giant trees
to deliver the
message)
here the minutes change
the light and dark on the faces of the islanders
and the weather never keeps

there is only this brief time
of birds and brightness co-mingling

on such a dawn
my mother saw Easter
moving from the other islands
closer and closer and
the saints and little people
left their caves
to welcome the long pink streamers of sun
and sang their combined gratitude
It never rained on Easter my mother said
My feet feel the searing bite in this delicate
ocean
I can only walk a little way.

On a hill dotted with grey rocks and sheep
another cousin welcomes us
his house is small and thatched
with windows beaded into the walls
as an afterthought
he is like my father
he is always building
his new house a concept
wistful and porous he has
worked on for years.
He remembers his visit to Canada
fresh from the boats   and everything
too large to think about
Maybe  he says  I don't want to build
maybe it should stay the same
There is strong tea and china cups
and vanilla cookies
I ask our hostess if she
makes the scones and oatcakes
that darkened on our ancient stove
The store is much too handy now
she says
My cousin tells us how he shot a dog
bothering the sheep
the night before
I do not want this tale
it is alien to my synopsis
(celtic warriors
spearing the viking hordes
the severed heads tossed
down a well)
I would like to leave
My cousin reaches
for a passing cat
his large rough hand smooths
the velvet coat

he whispers in Gaelic to my mother
who responds with smiles
I am not part of the story now
not yet
but it is still continuing.

Christmas on the island
was not a present day
there might be oranges
jams and marmalades
sent from Glasgow
there was midnight mass
for the grownups
who held torches in the
black night
and walked in groups
toward the rainbows
A morning mass for children
a manger
with the bent statues
caught in inanimate
reverence
Neighbours visiting
and songs and stories
beside the fire
beside the filled glass

But it is New Years that is
out of time
in the turning of the calendars
the gathering of days
that will burst to a conclusion
the bonfires sending sparks
into the air
Winter is slowly dying
the year's work is done
there is no present now
no past
the glowing sky shining
on the costumes
the green disguises
circles and music and patterns of hope

there is nothing that calls us now
we stand outside ourselves
beyond any visible force.

There was a repetition to the island life
like the recurring winds
the blending of twilight rains
the sounds of wings from the skies brightening
The women worked to invisible music
the stretching of the wet cloth
the hands that pulled the wool like taffy
drumming the table
crying o ho ro ho ro ho ro
The gutting of the silver fish
the cleaning the placing
in the pierced barrels
the elongation of the day
the voices filling the salt air
o ho ro ho ro ho ro
And my grandmother at her cow
the pull   the rhythmic splash
the cow's hair soft
on my grandmother's hands
Seonag   Seonag
pretty one   pretty one

My grandmother now in her Canadian home
listening to the same tunes
her voice harsh
whispering with the music
the crackling record stops
her song keeps on
her fingers moving rhythmically in the chair
deep blue as the night ocean.

## celtic art II

In this panoply I watch
there are forms that
cling to each other
the ones under the
ground
giving themselves to the sea
repeat their lines upon
the living
who speak to them
in perfect trust
and the sky is full of
signs
the clouds that touch
each other and break and
reaffirm themselves
in new reflections in the sea
light
and shadows change
in formal patterns   intertwined
held together under and above the earth
On the island there are no empty spaces.

The druids and picts sleep in their conical mounds
The vikings are appearing

Digging into the lines of the land
the archaeologists call up a village
The vikings though are not elusive
their names cluster the island
Brevig   Borve   Bentangaval
And Kisimul's galley
patterned its quick predatory lines
after their savage ships
The scientists are precise
there is too much to be measured
the possibilities stifling

I walk the old Peat Road
which empties itself into darkness
the Bochan path
home of the restless ghosts
they will appear and disappear
they are with me now
I feel the certainty of motion
their forms shrink into the heather.

The island men followed the sea
fishermen   mariners
after the monks   the saints
the pirates of Kisimul's galley
the smells of tar and canvas
enveloped them
called them to worship
as the incense of the mass
their creator held the stars and storms
and charted the great prows
that dug into the ocean
They came home exultant and fearful
They were not needed
the women had organized the island
the sheep   the cows roamed content
the potato crops risen in their trenches
and when the rains came
the fires lit   the peat readied
the fish salted
the cloth woven into a maze of colours
no beginning   no end
The women greeted the men
their iron faces softening
their eyes watchful against
excess disruption
they had conquered the grey dawn
the rolling sun
Long before the suffragettes
marched with their slanted ribbons
into the headlines
the island women carved
the seasons with their own hands
on their own terms
in the solidarity of the elements.

In the discussion of the thirties
my mother stands at the door
and the men with no faces
tell her their story
they have come too far
they have stood in too many lines
they are grateful
for coffee and a sandwich
They have snapshots of their homes
brief linear pieces that float and do not fit
They stand against prairie barns or
vacant wheat fields
their parents fade into grey walls
My mother listens
There were tinkers in the old country
homeless and nameless
in rags with bells that
rang before them like lepers
they were the poor souls
who were fed and
arranged among the heather
they were lost like
Columba's creatures
in a storm
There were more of them now
In the depression
my grandfather
walked toward the mountains
carrying turnips and potatoes
to trade
and men dug eternally in the same ditch
The letters from the island
filled with foam and rain
and dying fish
The world was standing still.

The second war was
filled with destruction
that I did not perceive
on the Inlet boats
which were readied
standing on the perfect platforms blocking the mountains
everyone had work
No one near me slipped away
(a distant cousin on the
shores of Normandy   the father of
a friend in Italy)
the skies were filled with paper airplanes
I knew the shapes the prisms
the radio proclamations
I was not involved
But my parents were--in their imaginations--
there were letters from the Island--young men at
sea and bodies washed ashore
and strange lights dancing over the ocean
and the clash of
viking swords and fires on the hills
My father home from the shipyard
slipping off his knit socks
his feet white and delicate
the veins bulbous
and my mother reading aloud
the last letter
the chanting of names
James and John and Ian and Murdoch
and all the young men
sons of their fathers
going down in the ships.

Inside the cottage
the pipes
matching the light electric feet
of the dancers
and the Islanders share the Gaelic
the young people switching
like transforming seals
from one language to another

In my childhood there were constant
gatherings
as the nights
ceremonial at the start
responded to my father's whisky
with increasing clamour

The whisky turns to story
my grandfather's garbled
indignant tale of Mary Queen of Scots
opens the old wounds
is linked somehow to the Bonny Prince who
led the clans into oblivion
the only common thread over two centuries
the treachery of the English
the hated Sassenach

And then the dancing
my father's ancient melodium
the ladies in their stocking feet
the men with rolled up sleeves
the reels   the night
in crowded circular movement
mountains disappearing upon the rain
the dances cease
my grandfather does not
alone in his tilted ship

he celebrates his hornpipe
sits down to frenzied applause

A cousin sings his own song
the emigrant
torn from his home in sorrow
they are all silent now
there are tears
not for ancient history
but for their island
the dead who have
not followed them
the cottages where it was always spring

The gathering concludes
my grandfather
inconsolable   heavy with loss   with contending spirits
tumbles towards the ditch
in the pelting rain
murmuring   it never stops

By tomorrow he will be
in his garden
the ripening plums
the texture of the sun
the pears enveloping the trees
the dandelion wine escaping
from the vat
he will dance along the rows
of cedar and roses
while far away the belligerent clouds
gather and rest
over the mountaintops.

There is a feis   a fair
and painted booths that flap
like seagulls in the wind
there are bagpipes and dancing
Gaelic classes and sombre
academics from Edinburgh who
come to feel the air
they do not smile   they seem aggrieved
because the centuries have turned over
there are Americans in new kilts who
are searching the shores for their roots
and bemused shop keepers who chatter in
Gaelic to each other
and smile appropriately
they are not fooled   the Gaels
their wry jokes make no sense
to the incessant pilgrims

I watch the dancing
there are young men in flying kilts
dancing the Highland Fling   the Sword Dance
I know the steps
briefly loved my moment on the stage
the kilts   the leather ties
the great wooden swords I carried upright
like small totems

Watching these savage leaps the
explosive attention of these dancers
I know my music was peripheral
this is where it belongs
in this ancient landscape
by this castle

There are torches now in the night
Kisimul's galley quivering from the raid
the triumphant soaring   the great hall
and the harp's fulfilment
weaving out of history
the indulgent songs
of prayer and blood.

Each Visge: the water horse


The cottagers meet in the dark night
of the peat fires
and stories are told
or chanted
repetitional as
responses at a mass
and everyone joining in
the tales are not fixed
they rejoice in embroideries
delicate and subtle
full of knots and links   and hints of unusual windings
So the giants roam
heads lost in perpetual mist
or the little people
industrious among the flower bells
or the dread kelpie the water horse
travelling the sands half submerged
(the faces in the cottage cleansed by
growing daylight
there are nods of recognition)
He is known to steal children   taste their blood
One in human form courts a girl
but killed by suspicious brothers
reverts to his own shape
iridescent in death
blackened by the moon
he will not disappear
with the rising of the peat fires
with the incantation
on the long nights
the water horse set free by words
will mount the sky again
eaten by clouds
and segments of dead stars.

Tabbar Nam Buadh  "the well of virtues"


In a white robe she stands
before the well
drawing water   washing away
the evil eye   the witchcraft
of the small harmful people
her hand holding the red flower of certainty
a light rain falls
May is overflowing
streams dissect the hills
the spirits are at their posts
in rivers and springs
she touches dew
that beads upon the hills
giving clarity and comfort
like the vernal grass   sweet
in the hollow of glens
She is prepared for spring
She will go towards the altar
while the beat of wings
the seals' song accompanies her
There are no footprints in the grass.

The woman in the kerchief
stops my mother after church
she remembers my father
he was a boy   she says
always merry
rushing with eyes that
were full of glee
she looks at the sea
coming and going
it is sparkling now
the distant slanted cloud
has not arrived
my mother did not know this boy
they were strangers on the same island

I think occasionally
I have known him
In my father's old house
my parents wedding scene
he is hand coloured   astonished
smiling amid the faint erasures.
Everybody loved him says my aunt
she points out the windows he set in
the small panes are sprinkled with rain drops
one slat uneven
(our house full of impatient signature flaws)
In other pictures he is aging
coming closer to me
we are both wearing
furrowed brows and distant eyes
he has given me his weariness
his insistent certainty
of possibilities.

Compton Mackenzie the writer
who brought patrons   celebrities
to admire
the island's teeming simplicity
lived his last years
in a stone house   not far
from the gravestones
the monks cell
above the immaculate sands
where planes come and go
at low tide
His life was full of manuscripts
siamese cats   and the company of
Colum Johnson, the story teller
weaver of tales
as intricate as the notes bursting
in improvisation
from his pipes
He was both friend and acolyte
The old men shared their lives and left together
Mackenzie piped
to his burial by Johnson racked with cough
the rain open and freezing on the grave
he would soon follow
They lie beside each other
in perfect harmony
with rain and pleated wind

The islanders talk of them both
their memories
Compton Mackenzie's words
   rigid on library shelves
Colum Johnson unfettered
   by print
his stories extending in trills and vibrations
throughout the island.

The woman knits sweaters
they have intricate celtic lines
colliding with one another
in continuous pattern
her husband   an historian
knows the island secrets
their cottage looks towards a loch
so small we would think it a pond
(yet in my photographs it is immense)
In the centre is a ruined tower
that has no lower door
you saw your enemies before they saw you
and so they circled
climbing to get in
It is half gone  the historian says
but more blood than stones have fallen
from this tower
the cottage fills with flowers and chintz and music
We tell each other names
they are the same
And so we smile
I could be here like them
knitting up history
with the broken violence outside.

On hot days the fog
rises
(the druid sea god Manamman
spreading his cloak
over the mountain tops)
a magic lantern show
translating mists into shapes
giant mushrooms soar
the standing stones have no substance
float without anchor
I think of the hoodoos in the dry country
in Canada
this soft island too is jagged   painful
yet unlike the sculptures
that are dead and permanent
the island will return
our boat moves in
wisps evaporate
the trail of the spirits darken over
a new population is hovering.

There were seal heads   bald old men
bobbing in the water
the artist sketching was trying to
hold them quiet on her paper
I sat beside her on the delicate white sands
and watched the ocean transferred to
her pad
a stab of lines the resting roundness of
the rocks
and the heads appearing as they would
from a magic drawing board

The seal people lived forever near
the Island
were transformed  at will
a story says a fisherman
angry at the bruising sea
lashed at a seal with his oar
later on land as he made his way through
the indented paths   over the hills
a hermit stood in his way
his beard was seaweed and a huge
cut ran across his forehead
the fisherman knew he had defiled a seal
and out of his contrition wept quietly
and the hermit enveloped himself in a mist
giving way to thyme and sea pink
  the artist leaves her sketch
  the light is changing   wisps of grey and black
  sunlight
  it is never still she said.

An island off my island
diminutive   uprooted in some other time
now joined by a causeway
that takes the tourist
backwards into that time
The island was bought by the gentry
who never owned it
Their Victorian house splendid and irrelevant
looked over the cave of the beheadings
(a tyrannical widow from the castle   from some other country
in the twelfth century
whose life was filled with disposable people)
Staring from their mansion the Victorian
owners
saw only desolation   felt only the
constant wind   sharp
the rain that seldom stopped
their silver walls could not protect them
and so they left
and the island now reclaimed by the Hebrideans
as was their story
They built small thatched cottages
surrounded by the other inhabitants
who had kept their distance
the people of the celtic fort
who filled the air with small chants
the vikings leaving the longboats
in friendship
and the little dark people
standing at the doorways of their burial cairns
silent   watching.

To accommodate sheep they were turned out
It was the nineteenth century
The landlord of the island
eradicated crofters one by one
(they were foreign
spoke a strange unwieldy language)
and there was smoke
and the thatched roofs crackling
and the sounds of
war with
swords and bayonets pointing
at the women in
shawls and men looking back
the whole hillside exploding
and the houses flickering until
they went out
and only the stones were left
cairns and crosses
taken by the sheep to shelter these
Columba's creatures
(who by this century did not
understand)
and yet it did not end
the remaining crofters
hidden till the great boats
sailed to Canada
who would come out to pray
to fall
upon the blackened earth
and then to rise again
to captivate the sheep
to build stone upon stone
in another part of the island.

At the outmost reaches of the Hebrides
there is an island
so remote
it has fallen through the lines
at one time a lost people
roamed the island
five families
living their lives with names
taken from the colour of sea and sky
and rainbow
practising an ancient religion
so old that visitors in the sixteenth century
were greeted with a sunwise circle
their chants and dances
echoing the swirling chaotic
sea
the island like a castle striking the sky protecting them
there were cattle and sheep
and grain that followed the dictates of
the sun
there is no one any more
their stones   the great thrust of the seamless circle
could not save them
there were thieves who
stole their food and then their seasons
their bodies
found by the cliffs
gathered at the edge of the world
waiting for the ship
unable to pierce
the circular storms
to preserve their century.

When the great ships which had crept towards Europe
were replaced by planes
and time became hours
the children of the children
visited their homeland
carrying messages and pictures
over the floating isle
and stories to be returned
The oldest did not go
they did not need to authenticate
the portraits
they knew precisely the sweep of sand
the stone houses   the unchanging people
they received the news with gratitude
and the children of the children
saw themselves over and over
the great grand daughter viewing with delight
the grandchild of the father's son.

Stone forms this island
underneath   above
there is grey rock surrounding me in this church
and old women in kerchiefs
and men in their dark suits
We stand out in our vivid colours
but our faces blend with theirs
we could move anywhere here
and exchange ourselves

My childhood church was wooden
(the sky at home filled with timber)
trees whispered when
the rains came
a soft harmony that echoed the waves
on the ocean's arm   so protected it
rarely sang

Here (as in my childhood)
the women sit up front
the beads on their rosaries
gently separating themselves
at the back the men   the young people
blinking in the slanted light

My father in my old church
always claimed the back seat
with other sleepy Hebrideans
he was full of sly wit
    irreverent asides
solemnity brought out the
    worst in him
and muffled laughter crept up from the back
while my mother at the front
        stared straight ahead
        at the statues

and spoke to him afterwards

He was unhappy at novenas or processions
With formal recognitions

I have a vision
my father newly arrived
at the seaside cottage
(uncluttered by youth or work
leaving the hated city)
while we explored the waiting rooms with bursts of laughter
my father on his knees in the bedroom
his head bowed   alone
thanking the god who had followed
        him to Canada
for the gift
  of this last ocean.

At the edge of the island a
stretch of white sand
where airplanes land at low tide
and nearby the old graveyard
I walk in the winds and a
slight sideways mist
and I am at home
this is no gated cemetery
this one is inhabited   flows to the sea

Here early monks built their
tiny chapel   built and rebuilt
in the beehive mound
an altar slab and stones that
hold up moss   and each other
stone upon stone

Among the celtic crosses
my grandfather lies
I never met him
there is only one photograph
he has my father's smile
his aversion to light
his hand blocking the sky
on that brown day

He filled the island   I am told
with whimsical tales
took books into the hills
and conjured lines
that sang in recitation
bird song   wind song

I trace the celtic cross
the swirling indentations
I know my grandfather now
we are chroniclers
in the same narrative.

In the book of the dead
my grandmother
who wore her skirts long
and rolled her hair into a net
who kept a sad mongrel dog
and teacups with tender patterns
brought out for every visit
who read Gaelic prayers
in the thick half light
caged by asthma and
the agony of migraines
who kept stands of leather books
the gold edges brilliant in the bleak room
whose fierce intelligent eyes stared into mine
she read me letters from the island
presented pictures of strange people
who were never in style
The pictures fluttering
like Alice's cards
the melancholy record
repeating itself
in Gaelic
till the needle sticks
and over and over
in the stuffy room
where the dark illnesses
are banished
a word is repeated
My grandmother seemed
preoccupied
with things that had
crumbled or left
the present in
the seamless past
the still browning people
with their bodies lost in the sea and heather

their documents
I wanted to comfort her
I did not understand
how content she was
like the other old Islanders
in their two worlds
how at gatherings
in their comfortable chairs
in houses with indoor plumbing
they would lean towards each other
murmuring their gratitude.

There were always foreshadowings of deaths
At any time an Islander
might be thrown from the road
while an invisible funeral
made its way into the future
one stood and blessed the premonition
that always came true
The dead lay in their own beds
devoid of makeup
around them a babble of mourners
conversing with them and
holding their hands
Good night   they whispered
Euche Vale

Later there would be drinks and songs
two men to keep watch through the night
with whisky and endless stories
while outside the sea and sky emptied
themselves into daylight

My grandparents in their new land
lay in satin baskets
they looked overbright
like the garish statues of the old church
they were buried by rote
the mountains indifferent to the plastic
lawns
But the sea remained
and always a piper spun the air to let them free
They had loved their two countries
They had come too far not to return.

The island men lived on the sea
My grandfather's story of his sailing days
climbing the masts while the wind
played its tricks   sweeping grey foam across
the decks
or lulled to a quiet that was more
frightening   the ship deserted and impotent
in the stillness
My father's stories
ignored the quiet times   the silent watch
they were filled with rushing danger
he joined the merchant marine while still a boy
lived through torpedoing   holding on to
a log   his legs disconnected from his body
repeating the Gaelic prayers
and hearing around
the drowning of other men
the fights in scarlet seaports   the saints and
criminals he overcame
the sea spray clearing his mind with its ferocity
(there was news from home
of funeral processions   wakes and shawls passed
around
they were far away   he said)
In foreign ports   he played the pipes
his cap filled with unrecognizable coins
his face set toward the next encounter

I think of my father as we row
towards the castle
I think of the galley that lay beside it
the men always alert
the raid on English ships
the great bonfires on the hills
and the harp playing tribute to the tale

And my father in his last years
leaving the city for the ocean
the view   he said   exactly like the island
racing in his small sailboat
only in stormy weather
coming back out of breath
his face shining
and I think of the heart attack   the warnings
his climb up the steep hill
along the trail of firs and cedars
in front of him the whole ocean
his boat   the Island
the heightened moment
of stillness
and his story completed.

The hill is dotted with daisies
that trample the grass
from the top the ocean can be seen
only fitfully
as summer breathes out mist
a ship is pulling another island
we find a standing stone leaning toward us
another has fallen   lies like a grave marker
scripted by moss
there is an abandoned hut and a dead sheep
the stones have seen the dark people
the vikings   the return
of Kisimul's gallery   the pillage   the celebration

My mother's house was once below the hill
she shows us small indentations
the site is devoid of meaning now   dead
as the sheep   the meaning of the standing stones
I photograph my mother   white in the light
measuring her lost garden.

We circle where my mother's house stood
and watch her watching
to see if anything moves
but only the wind floats the grass
and a cluster of rocks melts into the ground
It was like this she says here and here
I see the stones pulling together
the huge hearth
the iron skillet the pot thick as the winds
holding out the air
the spirit dew

Above the outline of the standing stone
we look up   there is some difference in our eyes
the time of my mother's house has swollen
bringing in the ancient signs
our presence
the shadow of the standing stones
coming to rest on the open door
we are here now
we are following the story.

In this history there are only assumptions
the island has enlarged
there are three houses which become a village
the tiny loch exhumes its growing castle
a clump of trees become a forest
and though I see myself time and again in these people
I am losing my compass
we are melding into one
The fishing fleet   my parent's home
the highland cattle   the songs of
my grandparents
the triumphant gardens   all are gone
as are the immigrants who
left for the new century
and I can not enclose it
It will be only in the air   flying home
that I can see
the island disconnected before the dawn
is joined to other islands
there is an ocean clipped
to the mainland   itself an island on another ocean
and somewhere between Europe and
America on the route
of the vikings
the celtic wanderers
with time going backward
I can simplify
my visitation.

I stand at the ship's rail
they are seeing me off
they are all there the
celts   the vikings
and the cave opening slowly to the sun
over the hills a rain cloud
above Columba's image
I am with part of my family
the missing ones wave
doors open   the generations
appear and disappear
separated from the visitors
who do not have their lives
the ship pulls out
the last the first
my people now grown smaller
folding into the sea
There are signs in the
promises we have made
slowly assembling
like the dig of the archaeologists
who have reached
the lower edge
the black hole
of the little people
they are looking up through the dark
their history like mine
has just begun.